A special Thank you to my husband, thank you for your continuous love, support and encouragement that pushes me to be the best me... To apostle Anita page, thank you for allowing Yahweh to use you to speak a word that inspired me to take my writing a step higher. Remember you prophesied (Erika you don't just write but you speak volumes). Also to those that supported me Daphaney, Jakita, and my big sis Nicole you are all appreciated

To Yahshua be the glory forever

This book is dedicated to my son Malachi, rest peacefully sweet baby I'll see you again; as well as my dad in law

The issue of blood: Woman man be made whole! Luke 8:43-48 King James Version (KJV)

43 And a woman having an issue of blood twelve years, which had spent all her living upon physicians, neither could be healed of any,

44 Came behind him, and touched the border of his garment: and immediately her issue of blood stanched. 45 And Jesus said, Who touched me? When all denied, Peter and those that were with him said, Master, the multitude throng thee and press thee, and sayest thou, Who touched me?

46 And Jesus said, Somebody hath touched me: for I perceive that virtue is gone out of me.

47 And when the woman saw that she was not hidden, she came trembling, and falling down before him, she declared unto him before all the people for what cause she had touched him, and how she was healed immediately.

48 And he said unto her, Daughter, be of good comfort: thy faith hath made thee whole; go in peace.

Table of Contents

Chapter 1
The issue!

Our bodies are full of issues and problems that are waiting to be resolved and waiting to be healed. We are walking around with infirmities known and unknown. Like the woman with the issue of blood, we go to therapy and psychiatrists and some seek psychics and worship other Gods. Some meditate to drive out the infirmity that has been there for quite some time, only to find out that it is still among you. What is your issue, what is your infirmity and where do you need healing? When she touched the hem of Yahshua's(Jesus) garment he said woman thy faith have made thee whole that means there was more to this infirmity, there was more than her just bleeding, she was bleeding out pain and defeat, she was bleeding out hurt and despair and things that were deep within that only she knew! Many of us have something so deep that is going on with us that no one can touch but the healer. I remember losing one child and thinking what could be wrong with my body, am I broken, am I a mistake because not only did I birth this baby and she passed, I birthed out another years later and he passed as well. I was left thinking something had to be wrong with me. Doctors tested me for everything to see why this may have happened, even though me and my husband had a daughter and the pregnancy was healthy and went well, I wondered why I lost the other children. And that was my infirmity for years. I believed I was broken for years. I believed my body was a mistake and some things were broken on the inside. Like you, I had many questions that led to other questions. My mind needed to be healed. My body was crying out for healing and for the master's touch. I needed healing for disbelief

and for thinking that something was wrong with me, I needed to be made whole. People were talking bad about me saying well she must not be doing right because this happened again. Ladies, there is nothing wrong with your body. You may ask why is this happening, why did I lose a child, why did I miscarry or why the stillbirth? You may ask,why? Does my body go into preterm labor? Some women may ask why can't I have children?I am sure that the woman with the issue of blood thought why have I been bleeding for so many years, I've paid doctors, I've done this or that and nothing is working. But there is a healer who can make all things happen and with him all things are possible! Don't give in to the enemy, meaning don't give in to the thoughts that this will never happen for you or that your body is broken. Women were made to produce and we were made to bear fruit. I don't care what the doctor said, what did Yahshua say?

Some people are battling issues in the mind or issues with the heart and we can't discover why we walk around with depression or anxiety. We are Left in a place of worry for no reason. Some of us fear the unknown or we fear losing... no matter what, these are all issues and infirmities and nothing is too hard for your Abba. He makes all things new! YOU WILL AND CAN BE MADE WHOLE!

Chapter 2
The Cell

I am sure that the woman who suffered with the issue of blood was left feeling alone; she felt she had to bear the pain on her own. That was a whole issue by itself. We sometimes feel we are alone and no one understands what we are dealing with but yet, I find that part to not be true because everyone is different, everyone deals with things differently and their pain may not be your pain. Some of us feel isolated in our own thoughts which only creates even more havoc, the important thing is to come out from the cell with your issue. I believe the woman became so tired of dealing with her issue that she sought the master out of desperation, she sought Yahshua(Jesus) out of a place where she was tired of going here and there knowing no one but him could help her! She refused to stay in the cell of her infirmities. It was time to really do something about it. Is this you?! I know it was me, I felt even though I had so many around me to support me I still felt alone. I felt isolated and I was locked up in a cell of hurt with many questions. When you're placed in a holding cell (jail) they give you a chance to make your 1 phone call. Some of us are calling on the wrong one. I decided that no matter how hard this issue messed with me I will call on Yahshua(Jesus). It was the hem of his garment that I needed to touch. Yes I had the support of my husband but he was grieving too see I needed to escape this cell. I needed the walls to come down. Sometimes we need to be alone to think and allow ourselves time to process, but do not isolate yourself too long, use your keys and unlock your cell. Your key is prayer and sometimes it's a silent prayer, he knows what we need.

Chapter 3
Cry out for help

How many of us walk around and act as if nothing is wrong? We go to work, school or home and we just go through everyday life and function the best way we know how. We choose to deal with our issues and infirmities by hiding them or burying them and never confronting them. We carry them on our shoulders in our minds and through our bodies. Which leads us to depression, self esteem issues, alcoholism and more. we become comfortable and some of us lie down in it. There are some who think it's normal to struggle or wrestle with what's on the inside. There are those who dwell in that place where we get in relationships and marriages and carry the baggage with us. We sometimes hurt those people along the way. We get intimate and pass our infirmities and issues on to one another. For example, have you ever met a man or woman who hurt you for whatever reason and it caused you to go out there and want to become a savage to others? That was me at one point before I got married. My issues within caused me to date one man but seek out another. Or my issue with losing a child caused me to think that every pregnancy could very well turn out the same if I have more. I remember how it caused me to worry about my daughter for no reason. See this is why we must confront those things that are there that are deep within because it will cause us to cry for help but not in the way we think it will cause us to do things we wouldn't normally do. I have met people who stayed within their comfort zones and

5

lived in a bubble because of their infirmities. which could be a deep spirit of fear, anxiety and depression. Some will never live out their dreams and follow them

because of the cry for help that was never heard because they chose for no one to hear them silently suffer. You went to doctors and allowed them to prescribe you every kind of medicine but you didn't seek out the true physician. Your life is nothing to play with, your reason or purpose to walk this earth is not to be handled so lightly. I have met those who say I want to heal but they continue to live within the place that's more comfortable for them. Some of you don't like to be the vulnerable one because you feel a man isn't supposed to cry or show his emotions. So you stay in a place that's most stable for you.

Some of you live in a place of danger, the dangers of hurting someone or never wanting to commit or communicate with your significant other. When will we sound off the alarm and cry out for help in the right way?! When will we talk about it? When will we fall to our knees and pray and admit that there is something wrong? There is an issue father and I am tired of it!

Matthew 14:35 And when the men of that place had knowledge of him, they sent out into all that country round about, and brought unto him all that were diseased,

Matthew 14:36 And besought him, that they might only touch the hem of his garment; and as many as touched, were made perfectly whole.

Chapter 4
Men who bleed

I had a dream about our black men.....in the dream I saw that they were working and sweating hard; and they were tired. I saw one white man standing on the other side as if he was watching over all the black men, like they were slaves. Then my dream shifted to me having my hand on my husband's chest and YAHWEH began to speak! The identity of our men has been stolen by white men and they never wanted to tell the black man who he truly was. Yahweh is saying to his men, take your KINGSHIP! YOU ARE KINGS! TAKE YOUR STAND AND TAKE BACK YOUR IDENTITY.... THEY ARE AFRAID OF YOU!

John 5:4 For an Angel went Down at a certain season into the poole, and troubled the water: whosoever then first after the troubling of the water stepped in, was

made whole of whatsoever disease HE had. John 5:5 And a certain man was there, which had an infirmity of thirty and eight years.

John 5:6 When Yahshua saw him lie, & knew that he had been now a long time in that case, he saith unto him, Will thou be made whole?

MEN STOP WAITING FOR THE WATER TO BE TROUBLED THE WATER IS BEFORE YOU AND IT IS JESUS(YAHSHUA)

You don't have to wait any longer until your redeemer is

here! Sometimes we depend too heavily on ourselves to heal on our own. (speaking to men and women) We wait for the season, or we wait until the time is right, but healing is now. o more suffering with those infirmities BLACK MEN YOU ARE NOT WHAT THE WORLD SAYS YOU ARE. FOR YOU ARE MORE THAN

CONQUERORS, YOU ARE KINGS, NOW PICK UP YOUR CROWNS AND WALK!

I believe as a wife that we should discern and we should always pray for our husbands. I remember when I was pregnant with our first son and I didn't see my husband break down and cry until he saw me and how broken I felt because of it being the second child I lost. I saw my husband cry hard and I looked to see him cry because this was the second time in 4 years I've seen him shed tears. That for me was an issue. He was hurting because he lost his first son that he really wanted. I saw him through his tears, we communicated emotion to emotion. He didn't have to say anything, his cry said it all; but it was more to this. Sometimes we hold things in for so long and we end up breaking down…some men hide their emotional side so well, until something happens to break it up then causes them to let it out….

The women's perspective

Men who bleed

I watched him go to work, come home, play with the children, talk to me, love on me then watch the game. Eat

8

and go to sleep. How would I have known that he was wounded? You mean you as his wife or girlfriend can't tell he's bleeding? Yes because we see no blood. He covers them with the best bandages he can find: The bandage of not talking about it, the bandage of hiding in the man cave, the bandage of playing with his kids. Pray and discern your wife! Don't badger or argue with him. Some wounds on men are easy to see. Wounds that would cause a man to not want anything to do with the child he has and walk out because he didn't want to be responsible for another life. We often question why a man would do this? Why are the statistics so high in this area with our men? Men suffer with insecurities that we as women know nothing about,

there is a weak side they cover up. What about when you see a man who goes from woman to woman and doesn't care who he hurts as long as his needs are satisfied? There are issues within him that haven't been worked out. Again he is insecure within himself. He hasn't been healed within, he feels comfortable with where he is mentally in his mind. But more so within the blood line what he's doing, feels ok.

Let's talk about the good man for a second, who's wounds are hard to see. the man who bleeds and no one notices. He would say well yes I have issues but doesn't everyone? It is different when we carry the issue of blood which is where we are most wounded. Some are walking around with a dad who has never been there or a wife who never appreciates them and talks down to him instead of talking

9

up to him. Some of us forget to build our men up and day in and day out we lose one, and not to death but to other things, like pride or silence where they don't open up. There are women who dog men out, use and abuse them and he leaves with spots of blood dropping to the ground. No one would ever know because they say men are not supposed to cry.

You would find some men who are wounded sitting in strip clubs watching a woman half naked dance and he thinks well, what's wrong with that? Shouldn't a woman show her body off? Ask yourself this, how would you feel if it was your daughter, niece or cousin?...Men with infirmities are also sitting in the churches.They are preaching, prophesying, and laying hands dangerously. Some are playing the keyboard or drums, some are singing, and if you discern well enough you can hear it in his worship. You can hear it in their preaching and instead of them sitting down and working through it they preach through it.... Men cry within as they bleed within.

Some are not afraid to expose themselves and talk with Yahshua. (Jesus) Some aren't afraid to seek out the physician to heal their wounds.. Men hide so well, they hide behind their suits and clothing and careers and even behind their attitudes. Before my husband, I dated a super nice man. He opened doors, treated me like a gentleman should but he did the same with the other 12 females he had lined up in his phone, and the main one who called my phone and threatened me to leave him alone. Again men hide well behind their issues which can cause many different reactions from them that we women would never understand. and We call them dogs and other names instead of saying I will pray for you even after he causes pain. We need to learn to walk away if we need to and pray. Men you need to know you can be made whole, you can cry, you can communicate. Will you step down into the water? Or will you continue dealing with infirmities and issues? John 5:7 The impotent man answered him, Sir, I haue no man when the water is troubled, to put me into the pool: but while I am coming, another steppeth down before me.

John 5:8 Jesus saith unto him, Rise, take up thy bed, and walk.

John 5:9 And immediately the man was made whole, and took up his bed, and walked: Kneel before the king man! Be made whole.

Chapter 5 \
Faith that can't be explained

As I layed down to talk to Yahweh, I began to shed tears and that is when I found myself in a place where I couldn't articulate or explain what I was feeling. I just knew that I wanted him to heal every part of me. It was based on my faith, it was based on how much of it all I believed. Truth is, I didn't believe I was healed because of me still being stuck in my past. I was haunted by who I used to be because of my own mind, and my biggest infirmity was fear. I feared the unknown. I feared that I wasn't truly forgiven. I thought that the father didn't truly forgive me. Yes, I thought that if things happened to me, like losing a child, that was punishment. My mind would race and that's what caused anxiety and panic attacks. That is when I began to speak about this woman who had this issue. She trusted Yahshua, she had what they call crazy faith. I would say her faith was big, it was unexplainable and that's the kind of faith I wanted. Any time you believe that all you have to touch if you can't get to him is a piece of his clothing or just the hem of his garment and you would be healed, that right there is strong faith. He said YOUR FAITH MADE YOU WHOLE. Because you believed that all you had to do was touch a part of me and be healed. The key part is she BELIEVED . We seem to live in a world that shakes our beliefs. It swirls with the spirit of fear, but, if our father who is in heaven says I haven't given you the spirit of fear but of power love and a sound mind. We should believe that! But we allow things that we go through to shake what we should believe. We have to get to a place where men shall not live by bread alone but by every word that proceedeth out of the mouth of

Yahweh! We have to get to a place where we believe that we have never seen the righteous forsaken, or his seed begging for bread. When are we going to REALLY get to a place where we truly BELIEVE that ALL THINGS WORK TOGETHER FOR GOOD TO THEM THAT LOVE YAHWEH? TO THEM THAT ARE CALLED ACCORDING TO HIS PURPOSE, o whatever happens in this life just know that if you truly believe good things are coming out of all you've gone through, it doesn't feel good but GOOD is coming!

Chapter 6
Wisdom, knowledge and understanding
Hard pills to swallow

How much are we praying that the father will be done in our lives? I remember being pregnant with my son and hearing at 11 weeks that there was no amniotic fluid around him. Doctors told me I should get an abortion or what they call a D.N.C but he still had a heartbeat I don't have the power to decide whether someone or anyone should live or die so I made the decision to let my baby live. I was not going to make the decision unless it was necessary or unless it became a situation where I had to actually take precautions to so if my life was in danger. So I chose to believe. I chose to have faith that the fluid would come back. I went from there all the way up to 19 weeks of gestation and still he had a strong heartbeat. He couldn't move around much anymore. He likely had problems breathing because there was NO FLUID but I kept the faith until I heard the words NO heartbeat after experiencing a cord prolapse which is the umbilical cord hanging out of me. The placenta was sitting below which was dangerous, I remember hearing the doctor read me the questions on whether I had a will in place in case I die in this process. I was so scared and didn't understand why this was all happening. I thought it was a dream, I prayed and prayed wanting things to turn around because that's how much faith I had. but Yahweh was saying I have your baby, I am holding your baby and this situation is in my hands so I went through with the delivery because the baby was already gone. I thought how is that my fluid didn't build up, how is it that I did all the right things,

I stayed on bed rest,stayed hydrated, drank a lot of water, and still my baby didn't stay alive. What I didn't know was that babies go through a lot when there is no fluid. It is a touch and go situation. I didn't know Yahweh was preparing me to go through this because I wanted my baby boy so bad. No matter what I didn't look at the possibility of how he was doing in the womb. Yes people have success stories with this situation but everybody and every baby and every situation won't turn out the same. We have to remain having wisdom and knowledge and understanding in all of our situations. We are to always have faith and it doesn't mean our faith has failed us, it hurts like hell to experience this but so much has birthed from me through this and so much old has died in me through this as well. I birthed out a new beginning and a new chapter in my life. I birthed a new pain that I thought I could never overcome

I birthed out a prophet who helped me to enter into my next level. I birthed out a testimony to help others because there are some who are bleeding pain and feel they can't bear.I come to tell you that you can overcome this, and feeling hurt, pain, and anger is normal but don't stay there, pick yourself up and believe again. Cry then believe again. Cry some more and ask all the questions as to why and then believe!

Your child is in the hands of the most high. He or she is safe with the father. They aren't sick, they are no longer suffering or feeling pain, yes we wanted them with us holding them in our arms but they aren't here, so through this I pray for peace concerning you. I pray for restoration concerning you. I pray you are able to be made whole, that you believe you can be healed and that good will be your portion.

You're going to have more children. Some of you feel you don't want to, some of you feel like you don't want your body to experience this again, but I dare you to believe and pray., just like the prophet told Hannah in the Bible 1 Samuel 1:17.

Then Eli answered, and said, go in peace: and the God of Israel grant thee thy petition, that thou hast asked of him. Get into your word and pray fast and consecrate that you receive the kind of faith this woman had. Even if you have faith as small as a mustard seed I pray you touch the hem of The master's garment and be made whole. Use wisdom in everything, gain more knowledge in all your situations and lean not unto your own understanding.

Chapter 7
The healing place

Jeremiah 30:17 For I will restore health unto thee, and I will heal thee of thy wounds, saith the Lord, because they called thee an outcast, saying; This is Zion whom no man seeketh after.

We often wonder how is it that we get to this place. They say all wounds heal over time but is that entirely true? Some wounds are so deep that it takes more than just time passing. I remember grieving for four years straight over my first child. I packed on excess weight, depression, alcoholism, and more because of her passing. It was not healthy for me because 4 yrs after her passing I met my husband and I still had broken areas. I was beginning a new chapter in my life and it was time to heal. Heal for good, specially because I was bringing a new baby into the world. Another little girl I had to be whole for, but mostly for me. There was a time when talking no longer helped. Going to church no longer helped, crying no longer helped. I needed Yahshua and before I welcomed my new baby girl he carried me to the healing place. I had to let go of anything and everything that was attached to my past. It didn't mean I had to forget my first little girl, it just meant I truly needed to heal. Being brought to the healing place is a time of reflection, a time of praying, fasting, and consecrating. Being Set apart from everyone. I had to come off social media, this time was solely with me and Yahweh and I had a reality check. I had to make up my mind and be at peace. It was then that I saw a new and whole me! I no longer cried, I lost weight and I prepared myself for a brand new chapter in my life. Four years later I experienced another loss

As I explained before I made it to 19 weeks. My body went into preterm labor with a cord prolapse and my baby was already gone. I found myself hunched over crying hysterically. How can this all happen again? I was in a new place in life so instead, I did something different. I didn't allow the enemy to kill me mentally or defeat me in this. I grieved, I was hurt, I was angry, I was devastated....but I grieved with Yahweh being in it(what do I mean?) I prayed and Yahweh gave me certain songs to play in my ears, he spoke to my heart, he told me to grieve but don't stay there in that place because I knew what happened to me before. I cried for my first son but I was soon at peace. I was at peace because I knew he was in the hands of Yahweh. I didn't know the Heavenly Father years ago when my Azalea passed away, not the way that I know him now. So now when he says I have your babies I find soooo much joy and peace in that. . I have found the healing place and it's truly in Yahshua. When you know him he will open the door.

Chapter 8
Somethings got a hold on me

I have seen issues within people that didn't want to let go. They didn't want to forgive the person who hurt them, they wanted to hold grudges because of what someone said or did to them 5 months ago or 10 yrs ago. It caused the issue of bitterness and anger and misery and they made others miserable. The issues of unforgiveness can cause many infirmities, the issue of not letting go can hurt you more than it hurts the person who did you wrong. How long will you carry that issue? How long will you hold your offender captive? When will you be free? Some have picked up chains and locked themselves up because they refuse to forgive. You are bound up and locked up within, more so than the one who's done it to you.Then, you wonder why you can't function in life and move forward; whether mentally or physically. Let it go, FORGIVE and release the issue that person has caused. Bag up and pack up every emotion every piece of hell they've caused and every hurt they've given and release it back to them. This isn't your burden to carry, they have left you with too many scars and wounds no more nursing the issue no more nursing the agony let it go!

The flip side

Somethings got a hold of me

You refuse to own up to it, you refuse to apologize. Learn how to own your mistakes, learn how to apologize for things you've done or caused in someone else's life. Sometimes you think you haven't done harm but that person's truth, that person's pain is theirs, within their heart. You are held responsible for how you've hurt them and if someone comes to you and explains this, that

this is what you've done and how you've done it they explain that for years. They've been holding on to what you did. Learn how to see things from their side, pray on it and get some clarity concerning the issue and deal with it! Learn how to listen to the matter even if it hurts or disgusts you. There are literally people walking this earth with the issue of molestation and they feel they have to live with this. They feel they have to live with this violation and assault on their body. You don't have to anymore, release it by helping others but first holding on to the master, even when the crowd is raging before you. When you feel you can't get to Yahshua,(Jesus) some days you feel like, well, I prayed and he doesn't say anything; we'll just call his name and believe by faith you are made whole and that you choose to live and not to die. This is what is caused when people don't apologize when people don't ask for forgiveness. You cause hurt, pain, and anger and much more within a person. It is time you confront who you've hurt and carry them to their place of healing. And once you've cleared your name FORGIVE YOURSELF. Don't allow you or them to beat you up about something you've cleared up. Don't build issues within you because of the past, forgive you, you are no longer held responsible even if they won't speak to you. Release yourself! We all have to manage to get to a place where we are not looking back. Everything in life is moving forward, not moving backwards. The days and months and years are going forward and Yahshua is doing a new thing. Will you be a part of the new?

Chapter 9
Bleeding out
Woman, man Be made whole

The more you hide the more you bleed, the longer you go on with living with the issue that's been hindering you, you bleed more. This woman bled for 12 years and some of you have been shedding blood longer than that, you've been burdened down with things for years. Some of you haven't been able to enjoy life the way you truly have been wanting to. Then there's the crowd who suppresses their issues by burying them in the wrong places within. When you should be burying them on the outside and into the ground. It does not belong in your heart, it does not belong in your thoughts, this is what's causing things like sickness and diseases. Sometimes this is what's causing anxiety and depression; YOUR ISSUES! This is what's causing you to make decisions that are not good, your mind is everywhere and some of you have been suppressing it for so long and saying you're free, but when it comes up or someone rehearses the past you know everything that happened word for word like it was yesterday. NOT GOOD, do you know there are things from my past that I can't even remember. Things I've forgotten about and when someone brings it up I'm like "really that happened?" Or I did that because I've truly let my past go. 12 years of pain, 12 years of being reminded everyday that this is her reality, 12 years of no healing and no help, but isn't it something how one

22

moment, one touch, caused her life to change forever? Yahshua(Jesus) was walking ahead looking forward and this woman was bold enough and determined enough that one way or

another she was going to get healed. Healing also begins with the mind, you have to first believe as she believed. She didn't say within herself well if I can just talk to him or if I can just ask him, she said within herself I'll touch his cloak, she knew the glory was upon him, she knew he was the true physician and the ultimate healer.

A word from the Author

Real talk, it does not matter what your issue or infirmities are. Go to the true physician, sit before him, lay at his feet, and let him remove every toxin, every inflammation and all unclean things that don't belong. He didn't design you to be sick, he designed you to be healed. He didn't form you in the womb to have depression or anxiety or hurt from the past. He didn't design you to cry your eyes out in the midnight hour because you're in pain. . Ladies, your womb is blessed and those babies are coming forth but one thing you must do is grab on to the hem of Yahshua's (Jesus) garment and grabway Hannah in the Bible. Lean not to your own understanding as to why certain situations have taken place in your life. Trust in him your Heavenly Father. Men you are special to Yahweh, we know that you cry though you may not show it. Some may need healing too, and we as women who lay at the feet of Yahweh should know. It is time we stop hiding and confront our wounds head on. We are bleeding out but we refuse to die in this. You have to refuse to give up, you have to go to see what's on the other side. There is a whole new life just waiting to begin, sin is also an issue and shall we continue in it shall we continue waddling and playing with our sin that grace may abound. Choose to surrender and be made whole. Choose that no matter what the crowd says or looks like, no matter what; trust and go touch the hem of His garment and be made whole man/ woman.

All things healed

When the woman with the issue of blood was made whole I'm sure she was able to go into places she couldn't go because of the blood flow. She was able to change her clothing, she was able to be intimate with a husband if she had one. She didn't have to pay money for doctors anymore. She didn't have to suffer or be in pain anymore. She wouldn't be talked about, she wouldn't be ostracized and most of all she could be herself again but new! And she would forever give the king glory because she knows where her healing came from. It didn't come from saging or chakra or meditation or worshipping other Gods. It didn't come from doing rituals. Her healing came from the king of kings, the true physician Yahshua hamashiac(Jesus Christ).

As I look at myself and the wounds from the inside out no longer appear. The bruises I once saw are gone, the people I once had issues with, there is now peace. Things are explained that's never been explained, where all hope is gone, there's been restoration. The blood is full of things that came from our families and ancestors. We have to become bloodline breakers just like the blood can carry HIV and other diseases. It also carries things that can't always be detected such as depression, anxiety, hurt, and unforgiveness. We can't carry on like this, change must take place and it starts with Yahshua. Call on him, let him clean up your issue of blood!

He went into the bloodline to heal because the issues and

infirmities came from within. Yahweh has reset things within you so you can begin again; you can start, over the choice is yours All things healed in your body all things are now healed in your mind. All things

healed in your relationships and all things are now healed in your friendships. All things are now healed in your marriage. All things are now healed within your single life. I said all things now believe it stand in faith and believe...

NOW POSSESS THE LAND!

Possess The Land

Duet 1:8 Deuteronomy 1:8 Behold, I have set the land before you: Go in, and possess the land, which the Lord swore unto your fathers, Abraham, Isaac, and Jacob, to give unto them, and to their seed after them.

Deuteronomy 14:2 For thou art a holy people unto the Lord thy God, and the Lord hath chosen thee to be a peculiar people unto himself, above all the nations that are upon the earth.

Chapter 1: The Word

You have heard from the prophets that now is your time; they have spoken over your life since you were a child. In your adult years, you've experienced things, made mistakes: you've been set free. You have been given word after word concerning your situation. You've been told things are about to change. You've been told that marriage is coming or that baby.. you've been told that job is coming or your family will be blessed. You've been given a word to stand or it's been said that the storm in your life will pass. And it is so! Everything Yahweh promised you it's coming to pass, his promises are manifesting and yes, and Amein his word is not slack. It does not return unto him void. You can take his checks to the bank and cash it with no interest, it is fully yours! His word is bond. Nothing the father says falls to the ground! His word is everlasting if he says your children will be free believe it! If he says I will open doors, believe it! If he said you are a prophet believe it! If he said he will give his angels charge over thee then believe it! The word is Yahshua(Jesus) the word is with him, the word is sharper than any two edged sword. Nothing can trump the father's word. Nothing can stop his word from coming to pass! You might have said well his word hasn't come to pass or hasn't happened yet, what's going on? I'm facing turbulence. Before a plane leaves it prepares for takeoff, you have to take your bags to baggage claim, things have to be checked and sometimes there are even delays. However, once the plane is ready for take off it is ready and that's where you are.You are ready for take off, the pilot has spoken and the word has been given about your destination. Then you will land and if it will be a layover. That's the true relationship with the father. When you go deeper in him

he will give you wisdom and sometimes destination times, or when turbulence is ahead .But you must go deeper and spend time with Yahweh. You must really give your life to Yahshua(Jesus) and never look back!

The Passengers Aboard

everyone can't take off with you. Everyone can't possess the land with you. There is much to possess and there's no room for negativity, drama, jealousy etc. Whether family, blood ,not blood or whomever. If they're not for you they can't go! What will it benefit you to carry all your luggage?(dreams visions ideas) and they don't help support. Be careful of those who sometimes do support but behind closed doors they're praying for your downfall. This is why you must grow your relationship with your father because Yahweh will expose what happens in the dark and give you much discernment. Everyone isn't happy for you. Sad but true! You will possess the land with those that are ready, those that have a mind to win, those who believe, those that are gonna help you and you are gonna help them. We must be careful of those we connect with and entangle ourselves with. Some are witches, some operate with witchcraft and some people carry the spirit of depression. No matter how many people preach or prophesy to them, they still want to carry misery with them. That is a spirit that has come to drain you! Be careful of the friend who loves to give you tea and gossip even when you say you don't want to hear it. Be careful of the friend who always wants to drag you out to clubs and parties. Be careful of the friend who always wants to shop and spend money but has bad credit. Those passengers can't go unless they're willing to change and get on board.

Purification

When you are going somewhere special or meeting up with someone important you shower and put on your best clothing. If they told you that you were about to meet the queen and she is presenting a gift to you that will sustain you for a lifetime, how would you go and what would you wear? Would you clean yourself up? How would your attitude be? How would your posture be? Hypothetically speaking if they gave you two weeks to prepare yourself for this what would you do? In order to possess the land you must purify yourself from the inside out. You cannot possess it in any kind of way; this is more of an internal cleaning. Your attitude must be right, it can't stink! You have to get rid of those selfish ways. You have to become humble. Your mind has to come up higher, your mind can't still be stuck in the projects. What happens if you're moving into a palace with a dirty infested mindset that you had before you became wealthy? I've watched people do that and their lights would get cut off because they took their bill money and spent it on Jordan's or clothes. I saw people get evicted because they took and didn't use wisdom and pray before moving. Thinking they could afford something but paycheck went to buying weed and doing other things instead of saving. Wisdom and knowledge is needed when possessing the land which comes from the most high. I remember him telling me to read the book of proverbs when I had an issue of always talking back or running my mouth, especially on my jobs. I lost jobs because I had a mouth on me. I hindered blessings because of my mouth piece, we must be careful because what we think is cute on us could be our hindrance. We must allow the father to clean us up and he will help you. If you read in the book of Esther, you

will see that she and the other virgins went through a purification process before they could have a meeting with the king. I love to watch one night with the king because I believe that was the best depiction of what is a part of the purification process. We must fast and consecrate ourselves, that is most important,fasting causes purging. Which causes internal cleaning. It is the heart that matters to our Heavenly Father and the heart must be pure.

Listen, Plan And Execute

Take time to rest before it's time! Being on a rest is you retreating when soldiers come off the battlefield they need to rest and retreat. Your time of resting is Yahshua(Jesus) time to pour into you, it is your time to prepare your time for worship. This is the time you should be listening more than talking. You should be planning or allowing the plan to come to you. When you come off this rest,it will be time to execute possessing the land. Possessing the land is not easy, you truly have to be ready! Football players work hard all year to try and get a Super Bowl ring and a winning season. When a quarterback is on the field he must listen and watch what it is he has to do. He has to hear every play to execute and try to get his man to the in zone. There are defensive players and they have to block. Yahweh will send people to get you to the promised land. You just have to be in the position to listen. Your posture mentally and physically is everything. Believe it or not! You cannot enter in with fear, fear must be destroyed. Fear does not come from Yahweh, he gives us power, love and a sound mind. 2 Timothy 1:7, you are supposed to possess the land with just that!!! Possessing your land is your destiny, it is your palace experience. It is Yahweh, giving you the kingdom. Your heaven on earth moments, but also your will to be able to stand through anything the enemy tries to throw your way. That's why nothing unclean can enter in with you... it must be a great cleaning out and doing away with.

This all comes with listening, planning, and executing to possess your land to walk into your new, GET READY!

Enter In!

During my time of resting I hid away from everyone. I hardly used my phone and I turned on instrumental worship music. and I laid down with my prayer shawl over me and was quiet... I also would go to the gym and work out and I worked on getting my body healthy because I dare not be unhealthy and not be able to enjoy the blessings that are about to overtake me. I could feel the healing and deliverance taking place within me. I was ready to enter in! I got rid of any negativity, that means people and more who spoke negatively. I got away from miserable situations. Nothing and no one is going to hinder us from entering in. This is the mindset you have to have. Are you really ready to enter into your promised land?

Royalty

You are free

You are new!

Your mind is free!

You are peculiar!

You are doing things you weren't able to do! You are moving

You are conquering!

Nothing blocking

Nothing hindering!

Because of Yahweh you are getting the bag that people told you that you couldn't get. You are living on top, you are living the word and walking in TOTAL obedience. You are living your best life. Blessings on top of blessings. Yes the obstacles may come your way but you will jump over every one of them.You are blessed in all things, placed on your royal garments because YOU ARE About to possess the Land!